Seleria's Story

Before and After I Knew Him

SELERIA PERRYMAN

CSN Books
San Diego, California 92119

SELERIA'S STORY

Copyright © 2011 by Seleria Perryman

ISBN: 978-1-59352-317-6

Published by:
CSN Books
7287 Birchcreek Rd.
San Diego, CA 92119
Toll-free: 1-866-757-9953
www.csnbooks.com

Printed in the United States of America.

Table of Contents

Dedication

I dedicate this book first to the Father, Son and Holy Ghost, my mother Hazel Perryman-Johnson and my children: Marcus M. Jackson, Kirby Bruno, Jr., Antonio Demaret, Jr., Antonia Demaret and Seleria D. Cook.

I have dedicated this book to the Father because He loved me so that He gave His only Son Jesus the anointed One to die just so I could be free from the bondage of sin.

To my mother because she has been a very important tool in getting me to know just how loving and amazing Jesus truly is. He has always been important in her life and she has never failed to be persistent in trying to encourage everyone to believe in the power of Jesus Christ who sent the Holy Ghost who then inspired me to write this book.

I truly thank God for allowing my mother, His precious vessel, to raise up the woman of God He knew I would become while still in her womb.

As for my children, I thank God for the patience they showed me during the times I was not able to do for myself after the ordeal of being in a coma, and for being there during my many times of need.

Introduction

I know there are many books being written about how to hear, feel, know and understand who God really is and who Jesus is to the Father of us all. I want to share with you my personal story on how I came to know Jesus and the miraculous things He did in my life. I know God is real and is still doing miracles for us today. I pray as you are reading this book that you allow the Holy Spirit to minister to you so you will never again wonder, as I once did, about who you are in Jesus and who is truly leading you through this life. I want to testify about how much the Lord loves you and me.

2 Timothy 1:8-9 (NIV) says,

So do not be ashamed to testify about our Lord, or ashamed of me his prisoner. But join with me in suffering for the gospel, by the power of God, who has saved us and called us to a holy life—not because of anything we have done, but because of his own purpose and grace. This grace was given us in Christ Jesus before the beginning of time.

We are to live a holy and joyful life in the Lord. Please, receive this as a personal letter from Him to you. Jesus' love for us is so powerful that He sent someone like me back to this world to have a second chance to live a righteous life.

We are to become examples for others who are not saved. We are to show them, not just tell them how they should live by every word from God. They should be able to see Jesus through our lives. We are the salt and the light of the world. We are to show the world beauty from the light of Jesus, who is the light of the world and now lives within us. Matthew 5:13-16 says,

> *You are the salt of the earth, but if salt has lost its taste (its strength, its quality), how can its saltiness be restored? It is not good for anything any longer but to be thrown out and trodden underfoot by men. You are the light of the world. A city set on a hill cannot be hidden. Nor do men light a lamp and put it under a peck measure, but on a lamp stand, and it gives light to all in the house. Let your light so shine before men that they may see your moral excellence and your praiseworthy, noble, and good deeds and recognize and honor and praise and glorify your Father Who is in heaven.*

I pray for those of you who do not have a personal relationship with Jesus Christ because you may doubt what you encounter while reading this book. Those of you who are already believers will know that the Holy Spirit uses every method available for us to get the message out. He will lead and guide us in all truth.

> *But when He, the Spirit of Truth (the Truth-giving Spirit) comes, He will guide you into all the Truth (the whole, full Truth). For He will not speak His own message [on His own authority]; but He will tell whatever He hears [from the Father; He will give the message that has been given to Him], and He will announce and declare to you the things that are to come [that will happen in the future].*

John 16:13

If you just trust Him, He will counsel you as you read this book. If you have doubt in your heart, believe me He the Holy Spirit wants you to open your mind to receive Him as the author. The only person that's angry with you reading this book is the devil who does not want your mind renewed! John 10:10 says,

The thief (the devil) comes only in order to steal and kill and destroy. I (Jesus) came that they may have and enjoy life, and have it in abundance (to the full, till it overflows).

God is giving us a chance to choose to live a righteous life. If you do so, you will be set free from the bondage of your past. Do you know that God gave Jesus, the Messiah, all power in heaven and on earth? We are told in Matthew 28:18-20 (KJV):

And Jesus came and spake unto them (the disciples), saying, "All power is given unto me in heaven and in earth. Go ye therefore, and teach all nations, baptizing them in the name of the Father, and of the Son, and of the Holy Ghost: Teaching them to observe all things whatsoever I have commanded you: and, lo, I am with you always, even unto the end of the world. Amen."

If you find it hard to believe that Jesus would want you, believe me you are not alone.

I am here to tell you that I could not understand why He gave mercy to someone like me, but as fast as the thought came to me, the Holy Spirit answered with a question: "Why not you?" God chooses who He pleases.

"For He says to Moses, I will have mercy on whom I will have mercy and I will have compassion (pity) on whom I will have compassion. So then [God's gift] is not a question of human will and human effort, but of God's mercy. [It depends not on one's own willingness nor on his strenuous exertion as in running a race, but on God's having mercy on him.]"

━ Romans 9:15-16

He then assured me that the disciples where just as human as you and I. I then changed my mindset as to who I was in Christ Jesus. I am the righteousness of God in

Christ Jesus. Jesus gave us power to tread upon scorpions and serpents and withstand all the fiery darts of the enemy! Luke 10:19 states:

> *Behold! I have given you authority and power to trample upon serpents and scorpions, and [physical and mental strength and ability] over all the power that the enemy [possesses]; and nothing shall in any way harm you.*

The Word says for us to renew our minds. *"Let this mind be in you which was also in Christ Jesus"* (Philippians 2:5). I take all the Word of God personally because I understand that Jesus had the mindset of doing God's business. *"My thoughts are not your thoughts, neither are your ways my ways, says the Lord"* (Isaiah 55:8). I have been commanded to speak whatever words I hear from Him, and only what He says. I can only imagine how the disciples felt when they were commanded to go forth to those who did not believe and how the fear must have settled inside of them. They must have had thoughts of how they were not worthy enough. Good examples of this are Peter, who denied Jesus three times (Matthew 26:75), and Paul, who used to put Christians in jail (Acts 8:3). But some of the disciples did not believe Jesus was the Christ, who was sent by God, even though they were right there walking and talking with Him.

> *He that cometh from above is above all: he that is of the earth is earthly, and speaketh of the earth: he that cometh from heaven is above all. And what he hath seen and heard, that he testifieth; **and no man receiveth his testimony**. He that hath received his testimony hath set to his seal that God is true. For he whom God hath sent speaketh the words of God; for God giveth not the Spirit by measure unto him. The Father loveth the Son, and hath given all things into his hand.*
>
> John 28:31-35

Jesus informed the disciples, in advance, how to handle non-believers who refuse the Good News by saying,

And whoever will not receive and accept and welcome you nor listen to your message, as you leave that house or town, shake the dust[of it] from your feet.

≈ Matthew 10:14

I also said to the Lord, "Who will believe me, who am I?" Reader, the Holy Spirit is faithful! You will not be able to say to God on judgment day that you did not know about Him or who He is. As you continue to read on you will see what I mean when I say I am being led by the Holy Spirit to write this book. With God's help I am able to write to you. It has not been easy to write down the secret things in my life that have haunted me—not until God set me free and now He has allowed me to share them with you. God assured me that men and women will be set free from the bondage of their hidden past secrets of hurt and shame ranging all the way back to their childhood! Please don't assume this is just for women because there are lots of men who are in bondage from their past as well. Men have a tendency to hold on to their hurt and shame longer than women because they don't know how to share the pain and overcome the shame. Satan is angry now because he knows that some of you who doubt will believe and be saved after reading this book. He alone doesn't want you free from bondage and saved from the eternal fire. He knows that once you are set free, you are free indeed. John 8:36 (NIV) states, *"So if the Son (Jesus) sets you free, you will be free indeed."* I encourage you to continue reading and judge for yourself. 1 John 4:1-6 (KJV) states:

"BELOVED, believe not every spirit, but try the spirits whether they are of God: because many false prophets are gone out into the world. Hereby know ye the Spirit of God: Every spirit that confesseth that Jesus Christ is come in the flesh is of God: And every spirit that confesseth not that Jesus Christ is

come in the flesh is not of God: and this is that
spirit of antichrist; whereof ye have heard that it
should come; and even now already is it in the
world. Ye are of God, little children, and have
overcome them: because greater is he that is in you,
than he that is in the world. They are of the world:
therefore speak they of the world, and the world
heareth them. We are of God: he that knoweth God
heareth us; he that is not of God heareth not us.
Hereby know we the spirit of truth, and the spirit of
error. You cannot understand the Holy Spirit unless
you first get into the Spirit of God for a full
understanding.

We are also encouraged in 2 Corinthians 10:3-6:

For though we walk (live) in the flesh, we are not
carrying on our warfare according to the flesh and
using mere human weapons. For the weapons of our
warfare are not physical [weapons of flesh and
blood], but they are mighty before God for the
overthrow and destruction of strongholds,
[Inasmuch as we] refute arguments and theories
and reasoning's and every proud and lofty thing
that sets itself up against the [true] knowledge of
God; and we lead every thought and purpose away
captive into the obedience of Christ (the Messiah,
the Anointed One), Being in readiness to punish
every [insubordinate for his] disobedience, when
your own submission and obedience [as a church]
are fully secured and complete.

There are so many things I could share with you
regarding how I know Jesus, but these few stories I'm about
to share are much more important to me than others
because God manifested Himself to me on these occasions
I'm about to share with you.

God took me on a journey. He took me back to my
childhood to show me how He was with me from the
beginning. Allow the Holy Spirit to minister to your life

about who He is to you. I AM is the ultimate healer; emotionally, spiritually and physically.

While writing this book I'm praying that God will reveal truth to you. I do not desire to add to or take away from anything He has commanded me to share. I truly believe with the faith He has given me that this book is inspired from the Lord and He will not allow me to dishonor His holy Name by allowing it to be published without His approval. God knows the intent of our hearts and what our motives are for doing things. He intends this book to be for His Glory to be seen in my life and for others to know that their lives can change for the better for those who love Him. Hebrews 11:1 tells us,

NOW FAITH is the assurance (the confirmation, the title deed) of the things [we] hope for. Being the proof of things [we] do not see and the conviction of their reality [faith perceiving as real fact what is not revealed to the senses].

My faith is for this book to be published so you will find the true you in Him and be set free, allowing God to get all the glory.

For with God nothing is ever impossible and no word from God shall be without power or impossible of fulfillment.

—✐ Luke 1:37

Chapter One

Emotional Healer

*T*hank God for Joyce Meyer who has shared her story with the world. She has given me the courage to do the same. I was molested by a neighbor as a child. I must have been about five or six years old when it first happened. I don't remember how many times it happened. I just know it happened. I understand now that I am far from being the only person molested as a child, but knowing this does nothing to change how you feel if it is you.

I carried emotional problems from my childhood into adulthood. I didn't even know how much it had affected me until I met Jesus...

He lived in a basement apartment with a family member whose daughter was a friend of mine. He would send the other children to the store for candy and would tell me to stay behind. He would suggest to the other children that I was too little to go with them and that they would come back quicker if I stayed behind. He would then fondle me in my private area. I remember feeling very angry when I was alone thinking to myself. This man was not the only one to molest me as a child, others did too. I was afraid to tell my parents. Some of you, to this very day, have not told anyone about what has happened to you. As I got older I allowed this to happen because I thought men would like me more. I did not have a male role model to teach me what appropriate boundaries were between girls and boys.

My relationship with my birth father has disturbed me more than I thought possible. My sister and I would go to visit our father and stepmother every summer when we were young until we became teenagers. My parents separated when I was still an infant. I never knew them to be together as husband and wife. My father has told my stepmother that he knew that I wanted him and my birth mother together again. I was told that every time there was a problem. He would share memories with me about how much fun he had with my older sister when my parents were still together before he married my stepmother. My sister was two years old when my mother left. He never failed to talk about how he would take her to the candy store that was at the corner store and give her whatever she wanted. He did not understand it hurt me every time we would come to visit him and that was the only story he would talk about to us. If she was not there he would still tell the story to me as though I wanted to hear it. He never spoke about anything that he and I did together. As I got older, I understood that he had nothing to share because he and I did nothing together alone—at least nothing that I could remember. He would leave me and my sister with our stepmother every time we would visit him along with our stepbrothers and sister. I grew to love this woman who took care of us while he was away, but the anger I felt had nothing to do with him and my birth mother getting back together. I just wanted him!

My birth mother worked two jobs until my teenage years which did not allow her to be at home very much. My big sister was my babysitter; we are two years apart. I remember having affection from my mother when she was home. I remember her sitting and talking with us wanting to know how the day went and the good times we shared together just doing homework, watching TV or going places on the weekend. I remember when my birth father came home from work he would just eat dinner, take a bath, dress for the evening and out the door he went. I used to ask myself why I would cry every day he would leave. Now as a parent myself, I wonder why he didn't ever asked himself that question, so he could find out the truth of what was eating up my soul the whole time. He just wanted to leave and go to yet another family. He would always leave us at home with our stepmother when we would visit him during the summer. I can say now that my stepmother really took care of us while he was out playing house with another family.

I had four stepbrothers and one stepsister. I could remember when he would get ready to leave for the night. I would go ahead of him and sit on the front porch hoping he would stay home with me because I was the youngest girl left at home. I prayed maybe if he would just see me crying and hurting inside he would stay, but instead, he just continually got angry with me for crying. He would always ask with a frown, "Why are you always crying?", but it wasn't as if he really wanted to know. He would just reach into his pocket and give me some change, thinking it would make me feel better, but I knew it would only feel better for him to leave. It got to the point that I just didn't care any longer I didn't want to be there left at his home while he was away all the time. As I got older, I would come and stay with him for a few days and leave his home to stay the summer with my mother's sister who also lived in the same city.

I can remember I would see little girls playing with boys or men thinking, 'They're going to try to fondle them', so I would watch to see. I became paranoid and did not want anyone to go through any of their childhood keeping this inside because they were afraid of telling. Oh what shame and fear came with it! I can't remember any good days with my father.

I'm not telling my story to hurt anyone, but to help someone like you who is reading this book, so you can know that when I met Jesus and allowed Him to come into my life He healed that broken heart. For years from childhood I carried those tears I cried on the inside and the mental pain that told me I should be ashamed of what I did. I did not know the depth of the hurt I was carrying. I never knew true love from the opposite sex before now. I knew lust, not love. I don't believe my father knew true love from his father, so how would he be able to give what he never knew as a father? He always said, "I love you," but it never really touched my heart—just sounded like empty words. I never felt it in my heart. I pray and believe that now that I'm living in the same city he does that we will somehow find a path to bond, in Jesus' Name. This is my hope for me and my father.

I'm also writing to those who have molested children. I'm doing this, so they can also see through my life story the enormous effect they have on those being molested. I pray the Father which is in heaven to also forgive you too. I now understand that true love comes from God because He is love. *"He that loveth not knoweth not God; for God is love"* (1 John 4:8). The Bible also says that *God so loved the world, that he gave his only begotten Son, that whosoever believeth in him should not perish, but have everlasting life* (John 3:16). Jesus died for me yet while I was still a sinner. I know my Lord is faithful. I have now forgiven myself, my father, and the people who molested me. I pray they also forgive themselves, and accept Jesus as their Lord and Savior. I feel there is no need to give names; they know who they are and so does Jesus. Allow me to continue with my story.

Before I was able to forgive, I hated myself and did not tell my parents or anyone about allowing the boys and the men to touch me. I knew in my spirit it was wrong, but I thought it was love. Remember, I had not really accepted Jesus as my Lord yet. I decided to go all the way at age fifteen. I got pregnant and could not stop the cycle. I ended up having three pregnancies with a total of four children at this time in my life. One of the pregnancies produced twins. Each of the pregnancies was with different fathers and out of wedlock. I was looking for love in all the wrong places. I thought I was over all the pain from my childhood because I was able to hide it in the back of my mind and walk around with a smile on my face, but little did I know what is in the dark will haunt you!

In order to overcome things, they must be brought into the light. You must be free to live and know the true you... who God sees you to be. You cannot love anyone else until you first love yourself. If we obey and serve Him, we will spend the rest of our days in prosperity and our years in contentment. I knew this was only the beginning of the changes God was bringing into my life. I decided simply to obey Him and knew that He would do the rest. Remember I had not known Jesus yet.

I was now in my twenties living with the father of my twins who were the youngest of my four. I was working two jobs because their father got hurt on his job and did not work any longer. While I worked he stayed home with the children. I was not going to pay a babysitter while he was home. My oldest son informed me that while I was at work the twin's father would do drugs with a friend in the bathroom. That's when I realized that was where the money was going. One lonely night, I was sitting at home with my four children. They were playing contentedly without a care in the world. Only my oldest son knew what was going on at the time. I asked the father of my twins to leave the house after a fight that turned physical. I understood that I could not allow my children to grow up in that kind of environment! I knew things were going to get harder for us, if that was possible. I was already a few months behind on rent, lights and gas. They sent out final notices on every bill including the house phone. I had no food in the house. We ate day-by-day not knowing where the next meal was coming from. The building we were living in was sold to new owners and they wanted me out.

I had to quit my jobs because I could not afford a babysitter. Normally, I would call on my mother for help and she would gladly come to the rescue, but this time, God would not allow the provision to come from her. She was not able to help me financially. God wanted my attention directed at only Him. I now know God will stop others from helping you just so He can get your attention. I started worrying about how I was going to take care of my four children without a job or a place to live and did not want to ask other family members for help because I had put myself in that situation. I decided I didn't want to be on welfare again. My mother would always tell me to just ask Jesus for help. I would just take the phone from my ear; I didn't want to hear that! All I wanted to hear was how she could help me. I had faith in her; I knew she would do anything to help me and her grandchildren keep that apartment. Jesus wanted me to have that same faith in Him.

One night the new owner came to my home and asked me to be out of the apartment the next day. I felt I had nothing to lose, dropped down on my knees that same night, and cried out to Jesus for His help. I already believed in God, but had doubts about the Son of God. When I cried out to Jesus, I asked Him to let me know without a doubt that He was real and was the true Son of God. I asked Him to show Himself to me in some way that no one else could explain. I could not believe just by my mother saying, "Ask Jesus for help" that this was happening to me. My mind was so programmed from the world's viewpoint. I truly thought I was going against God if I believed in a Jesus who came as a man into this world. I did not know if He was just a myth

20

that ancient people made up or what. There are so many religions today. How could I know that my mother or anyone else was telling the truth?

I was fortunate to be able to go to work at my mother's place of employment. I began making telemarketing calls. Her boss was a young man who became a good friend of hers. He knew I was one of the worst employees he had ever hired once before! I promised him that I would do better and if I didn't he could just fire me. He gave me another chance. Once I was making money, I forgot all about the prayer I prayed to know Jesus. I thought I was doing fine and had worked it all out on my own. Even with my new job, I could not afford a sitter for the twins. My older children were in school and I was fighting a custody case for my middle son. I was trying to keep all my children together and worried about how I was going to feed them. I had to take the twins to work with me. We rode the train for two hours to get to work. I was getting desperate! My mother would leave her work to come and meet me at the train station which was a few blocks away from the office to help me with the twins.

Usually a week before payday, I would be very hungry. I made sure that the twins had snacks, but there would not be enough for me. This became a pattern. Even when I fixed dinner at home, I would not eat until I knew that all of the kids had enough. If the twins would ask for more food, my oldest son would get angry with them because he knew I had not eaten anything. I would give my portion to them and tell them I would eat something later. One day my cousin came over my house to visit and she noticed I had lost a lot of weight. All my clothes were too big for me. She encouraged me to buy some new clothes. I had just gotten paid. I had not spent any money on myself for a very long time and it felt good to take care of me for a change.

I had to work long hours. My mother did not have any extra money to give and I did not have a dime. I did not want her to know that I had not eaten anything that day. I started looking through my purse for loose change. I looked through every pocket of my billfold in my purse. My mother started to joke with me laughing and saying things like, "How many times are you going to look in that purse?" I knew that I had already looked through all the compartments and the checkbook several times. When I was about to give up looking and started feeling sorry for myself, a quiet voice said, "Look in your checkbook one more time." I did not know that it was the Holy Spirit talking to me because I didn't know His voice yet. I thought I was talking to myself. I decided to look one more time. I wanted a candy bar from the candy machine. As soon as I opened the checkbook, there was a brand new twenty dollar bill inside!

As soon as I saw that twenty dollar bill, Jesus spoke to me and said, "Here I am; now you know me for yourself." God had put the money on top of everything so I could not say that I had just overlooked the money. I know I did not have that money in my checkbook. I started to cry and praised Him by thanking Him for revealing Himself to someone like me who did not believe. My mother took me outside to find out what had happened. She knew God had shown me something, but she did not know what because I could not stop thanking Him. I then became afraid because I knew He was real. I started to think of all the sinful things I had done. I was outside trying to light a cigarette, and praise God at the same time. I could not stop crying, laughing, and jumping for joy long enough to tell her. I was sad for sinning, and excited at the same time because I now knew Jesus for myself. My mother smacked the cigarette out of my hand! She did not want me praising him with that cigarette in my hands because of respect for Him. That was the first time Jesus revealed Himself to me as my provider. For the first time, I was able to pay all my bills. I moved into a three-bedroom house and paid less rent than I was previously paying for a two-bedroom apartment.

Chapter Two

Spiritual Healer

I was now in my early thirties and had just experienced a divorce. I had chosen a husband myself without God's help. This is important to share with you because God wants us to wait for Him to send us a spouse. He is the One who knows what we need from another person. He never intended for us to divorce, but He is faithful to forgive us for our mistakes and sins.

> *If we [freely] admit that we have sinned and confess our sins, He is faithful and just (true to His own nature and promises) and will forgive our sins [dismiss our lawlessness] and [continuously] cleanse us from all unrighteousness [everything not in conformity to His will in purpose, thought, and action.*
>
> — 1 John 1:9

When I learned to hear God through His Word, things started to change in my life. I was learning to become obedient as I studied the Word of God. I had so many questions. I was not able at the time to understanding what the Holy Spirit spoke to me because it would be a spiritual conversation and I was still thinking with a worldly mind. *God is not the author of confusion* (1 Corinthians 14:33). The truth is, I was not able to fully understand because I was supposed to listen with my spiritual ears not just my physical ears. He wants you to know the true you—that person He knew you to be in Him.

I grew up in church all my life and was baptized as a little girl when I was eight. My mother always had us in Sunday school and Bible study and I was even in the choir at one time. When those doors of the church were open we were there, but I did not know Jesus for myself personally. I had only heard about Him. I was living contrary to the Word of God and had problems hearing his voice much of the time. God was trying to get my attention. He had already called me into the ministry years before I met my ex-husband.

Let's go back to when He called me to Himself. God called me to preach and teach His Word when I was living with my twins' father before I got married to someone else. I had already had two other children. Nevertheless, God still called me to Himself while I was deep in sin! God tells us in His Word that He knew us while we were still in our mother's womb. Jeremiah 1:5 states:

> *Before I formed you in the womb I knew [and]*
> *approved of you [as My chosen instrument], and*
> *before you were born I separated and set you apart,*
> *consecrating you: [and] I appointed you as a*
> *prophet to the nations.*

I did not know who I was in the Son of God's eyes or how He could care for someone like me, but God knew I loved Him. The Bible says that no one can come to the Father except through Christ Jesus, and no man can come to the Son unless he has been sent by the Father.

*No one is able to come to Me unless the Father Who
sent Me attracts and draws him and gives him the
desire to come to Me, and [then] I will raise him up
[from the dead] at the last day. Jesus said to him, I
am the way and the Truth and the Life; no one
comes to the Father except by (through) Me.*

John 6:44,14:6

Let's take a journey down memory lane. One cold winter
day, Jesus spoke to me while I was standing on a corner in
Chicago on the north side by the lakefront waiting for a bus.
It was about 7:00 a.m. As I waited, I heard a voice say to me
deep in my soul, "Study my Word and teach MY people how
to live by every Word of God." I said, "Yes Lord," even though
I was not sure if that was His voice. I said nothing to anyone
at that time because I did not want them to laugh at me. A
few days later, a Caucasian woman said these exact words
to me as I looked into her eyes, "God told me to come and
talk to you." I wondered why there was a middle-aged
Caucasian lady at the bus stop in a black neighborhood. She
started crying and began telling me her life story. She was
being abused and threatened by her husband who was still
receiving his deceased son's Social Security checks and was
an alcoholic. He threatened that if she told anyone he was
still getting the checks for his son he would kill her. I asked
her if she was a believer in Jesus Christ. At the time I did
not know the Word of God, yet, as I started speaking, words
that I knew came from heaven suddenly came out of my
mouth that was stored in me from a child. I know God will
give us the words to say when it's time. I urge you not to
worry if you can't remember everything you are reading at
this time, just keep studying the Word and He will bring it
to your mind when it's needed.

*But when they deliver you up, do not be anxious
about how or what you are to speak: for what you
are to say will be given you in that very hour and
moment, For it is not you who are speaking, but the*

Spirit of your Father speaking through you.

Matthew 10:19-20

I could not believe what had just happened! The woman and I were laughing and hugging one another. When the bus finally came, we got on the bus as friends and sat together and talked until one of us had to leave. That moment was so unreal to me! I would pray every night to see that woman one more time just to know if she was a person or an angel. My mother always told us to be careful of strangers; because we don't always know who we are entertaining...it could be an angel. God allowed me to see her one more time. She recognized me one day as I was leaving work. She said to me, "I was praying and asking God to see you again." She told me she was shopping for gifts she was giving to some of the people that had helped her while she was going through her ordeals. She told me that she had taken the advice that the Holy Spirit gave her through me. She had gone to a shelter. She was now saved and filled with the Holy Spirit! While she was buying gifts for the people at the shelter, the Holy Spirit told her to buy an extra gift. She said, "I kept saying to myself, "but I have one gift for everyone who helped me," but everything inside of her kept telling her to get another gift." When she saw me on the bus going home, she started crying, saying, "I prayed to see you again to thank you for everything." She reached into her bag and told me that she now understood why He (Holy Spirit) kept telling her to get the extra gift: "It is for you!" She was so excited! I can't explain the feeling I got from that encounter, but I do know it impacted me. I'm writing about her in this book for someone else to find relief in whatever God is calling them to do for His purpose.

I can truly say He knows us while we are still in our mother's womb. When I became a young lady I always knew I was different than my friends. I don't remember anyone teaching the Word of God like they do now. I was confused.

My only knowledge about preachers was that they flirted and cheated on their wives. When they were "preaching," there was a lot of yelling and "performance" I called it, but no anointing. Now that I know better, I did not want to be like them. I never told anyone that I was called into the ministry besides my mother and my stepfather; my stepfather did not believe in women ministers at that time.

One Sunday, my Sunday school teacher at Union Missionary Baptist Church, struck a match to the fire that burns inside of me to this very day. I would ask all kinds of questions and she would always find the answer for me. One of the deacons at the church was also very helpful to me. He once said to me is, "Don't ever let the fire I see in your eyes go out!" He said it with such passion in his eyes that that command will remain with me today and forever. He can't even remember saying it to me now, but that's because it was for me to remember. From that moment on, I was in Sunday school. Little did I know that the Holy Spirit was teaching me to hear His voice through others he appointed over me. I will also never forget another powerful woman, a young lady that I truly admire. What I saw in her was something different that I wanted deeply. She was superintendent of the Sunday school classes, and when we all would come together she would be the one who would provide the lesson. We all would be in one accord. I truly saw God in her when she would speak about Jesus. I was informed one day by God that I would be trained under her ministry. She didn't know who I was in Christ, she just knew my mother as a faithful woman. I called her one day and asked if she was called into the ministry to preach. She responded that she was not sure. I then started to tell her what the Lord told me about her. She just looked at me and smiled. I knew she thought this was crazy. I will tell you at the end of this book whether I ended up being trained under her or not.

I now know that everything the Lord tells you will come to pass. If it does not, then it was not of God. Deuteronomy 18:21-22 states: *"And if you say in your [minds and] hearts, How shall we know which words the Lord has not spoken?"* When a prophet speaks in the name of the Lord, if the word does not come to pass or prove true then that is a word which the Lord has not spoken. The prophet has spoken it presumptuously; you shall not be afraid of him. I will never forget these people as long as I live.

When I attended church services I used to speak only to the ones I knew. Anyone I really didn't know who was not in my little circle I had made for myself, I would act as if I did not see them or I would purposely try to avoid looking at them. Some of you reading this book know what I'm talking about. I would just come to be seen by my pastor, so he could see that I had attended. I used to pray that God would tell him I was called to preach. I was more interested in pleasing man than God. When we are trying to please man, we are in the flesh. Nothing in the flesh pleases God. I wanted to let my pastor know I had been called into the ministry, but I was afraid that he would not believe God would call a woman like me to preach. Little did I know that the enemy comes to steal, kill and destroy us and the ministry God has given us to do.

I found out later that God does not give us a spirit of fear. That spirit comes from the enemy! *"For God hath not given us the spirit of fear; but of power, and of love, and of a sound mind"* (2 Timothy 1:7, KJV). The adversary (a.k.a. the devil) kept on whispering lies to me. He is the father of lies. John 8:44 (NIV) says:

> *You belong to your father, the devil, and you want to carry out your father's desire. He was a murderer from the beginning, not holding to the truth, for there is no truth in him. When he lies, he speaks his native language, for he is a liar and the father of lies.*

Satan said things like: "You don't speak to all the people when you come to church; you don't know the Word of God; you don't even come to church every Sunday, nor do you pay your tithes all the time...who is going to believe that you of all people would be called to do God's work?" This is why we must do all God asks of us: love your neighbor, study to show yourself approved, be faithful, and give Him His ten percent. When you do all God asks of you, you can then say to Satan, "Get behind me, you father of lies!" I didn't know the enemy's tricks or the Word of God like I do now. The enemy comes to steal, kill and destroy us and our calling. The only way he can prevent the will of God to be manifested in your life is to get you to believe his lies. If Satan had the power to kill you, you would have already been dead while yet in your sins. But, God knows the plans he has for your life. Jeremiah 29:11 states:

> *For I know the thoughts and plans that I have for you, says the Lord, thoughts and plans for welfare and peace and not for evil, to give you hope in your final outcome.*

God had shown me that my Sunday school teacher was called to preach, but I could not understand what God was trying to tell me at that time in my life or why He would talk to someone like me who was not faithful at that time. I could not understand why she wasn't preaching if He called her.

God does not see us for who we think we are, He looks at our heart and knows all about us. He even knew how I was going to react when He called me. God is not surprised when we do foolish things. The Bible says that God knew us even while we were still in our mother's womb. The Holy Spirit is the one who does the changing from the inside out. If we were able to do it ourselves, then Jesus' death was in vain. We must give the Holy Spirit permission to work in us and surrender our will.

One Sunday, the evangelist taught on fornication. She taught women from ages eighteen to thirty. The evangelist would speak the reality that was going on in our lives. She would give examples from her own life, not holding anything back that she felt would prevent us from sinning against God. The Word of God convicted me so that I was afraid. I knew I had to change the way I was living. I knew that I could not continue to live with a man that was not my husband. I was having sexual relations with this man and he did not have any desire to marry me, but he didn't want to move out. All I could think about was that I was a fornicator since the age of 15 who ended up with four children. I carried that guilt around with me for about a year until I began to notice the change on the inside of me. Every time we would have sexual relations, I did not experience pleasure, but guilt and shame. I was angry about having children out of wedlock. I did not like that feeling and knew I had to do something about it. However, I thought it was too late for me to do anything about my life. That's when the evangelist taught on forgiveness. I was set free that Sunday! God is not the author of confusion, but of a sound mind. I believed God was talking only to me when He spoke through her. She taught about confessing our sins to God and how no matter how big the adversary tries to make the sin look in our eyes, God would forgive us. Not only that, she said, "He would not even remember them."

Thanks be to God for his Word and mercy! 1 John 1:9 (CJB) states,

> *If we acknowledge our sins, then, since he is trustworthy and just, he will forgive them and purify us from all wrongdoing.*

I went home and asked God to forgive me for all my sinful acts and to show me how to change my life. I'm now content with waiting on that special someone to come into my life to share the love of God. I know by experience that

God will show you how to be content until He sends the one person He has for you.

I knew then that I had to get out of that ungodly relationship with my boyfriend, but we all know bad habits don't change overnight. I acted as though I didn't hear the warning. I continued to live with him for a few months until thing got crazy. He had no idea what was going on inside of me. I also was thinking of my middle son who was staying with his father at the time wandering if he was okay and feeling angry because he wanted to live with me too. But that's for another book. When I look back, God helped me through that custody battle too. I finally asked my boyfriend to leave, but I did not want to tell him that this was God's idea. The truth is, he did not go to church and I was ashamed to tell him how Jesus was talking to me knowing the life I was living with him already was a sinful one. This is the man who is now my ex-husband. Before we married, I knew he did not want to marry me and I also knew he did not want to leave. Again, I tell you Satan comes to steal, kill and destroy. Just before he was about to move out, I received another blow. My sister, who was on drugs at the time, came to visit me and said that she was pregnant and did not know who the father was. Somehow, I knew that the child she was carrying was mine, but I did not want to raise another child alone. I was not trusting God to take care of me yet. God does not force us to do what He wants. He allows us to have use of our free will. However, He will plead with us to follow Him because he loves us and knows what's best for us.

God was patient with me and allowed me to make my mistakes. I could do nothing good without His guidance. At the same time, I was taught how to hear His voice above the adversary's voice. If you never have any trials or temptations, how will you know who brought you out of them? How can you even have a testimony? Our lives should be a testimony of all the mistakes we make, so the children of

God know they are not alone. If God did something for someone else, He will do it for me too. He is no respecter of persons!

I now understand that God does not play favorites,
but that whoever fears him and does what is right
is acceptable to him. No matter what people he
belongs to.

Acts 10:34-35, CJB

A few months later, the baby was born. My boyfriend and I took my sister to the hospital and she had a little girl. One night, about four weeks later, the hospital called me at around 12:00 midnight to inform me that it was time for the baby to go home. I did not know the baby was still at the hospital. The baby was in the hospital for about four weeks because she was premature and had traces of drugs in her system. My boyfriend and I got up and went to a 24-hour K-mart to buy things for the baby to come home in. The child welfare woman called that morning wanting to know if I could pick up the baby, since I was the maternal aunt. My sister had left without any notice as to how to contact her, and she never returned to the hospital. We did pick the baby up from the hospital, and my boyfriend fell in love with her. He still did not want to marry me, not because he didn't love me, he said. He was engaged to marry someone else before he met me and she left him, so he was afraid. The caseworker informed him that unless we married, he had to move out before I could adopt the baby. He couldn't stand the idea of losing her and agreed to marry me. The Holy Spirit advised me not to marry him, but fear stopped me from listening. I agreed to marry him and we went to City Hall. All my other children knew that it was a mistake. We argued all the time. I can remember when the judge asked me, "Do you take this man to be your husband?" The Holy Spirit spoke in an audible voice: "NO!" I was so surprised. I said yes anyway, I guess out of fear. I was speaking to the Holy Spirit, but the judge continued the ceremony and I did not stop him like I should have. The very next day we tried to get an annulment from the court at City Hall and they told us we had to file for a regular divorce. We decided to give it a try. We both adopted our daughter and love her to this day! He is a wonderful father to her, but I cannot say that he has been a wonderful husband to me.

We were married for five years. He took drugs and was mentally abusive to me. He would hold our daughter and tell her how much he loved her and I would pray that he would love me that way too. It took about one year for me to seek God's face regarding what I should do to get out of the mess I made for myself. I knew that God would not be pleased with me for divorcing my husband, even though He told me not to marry him. I could not sleep. I was so depressed that I gained lots of weight. I finally sought wisdom from some of the leaders at church, but the final Word came from God. Once that happened, there was peace. When I made my decision, everything in my life changed once I got in one accord with God. I asked the Lord to forgive me for going against his will for my life and marrying the man He advised me not to.

In addition, I forgave my ex-husband. We became very good friends. God is faithful to forgive us. That is why it's important to know who you are in Christ Jesus. This is what the Bible says about who we are in Him: *"No, in all these things we are more than conquerors through him who loved us"* (Romans 8:37). *"For everyone born of God overcomes the world. This is the victory that has overcome the world, even our faith"* (1 John 5:4). *"I can do everything through him who gives me strength."* (Philippians 4:13). *"What, then, shall we say in response to this? If God is for us, who can be against us?"* (Romans 8:31). God healed me from all that emotional and spiritual pain. I thought it was in my hands and I could handle it, but God showed me how and He will show you too. Matthew 11:28-30 says,

Come to Me, all you who labor and are heavy-laden and overburdened, and I will cause you to rest. [I will ease and relieve and refresh your souls.] Take My yoke upon you and learn of Me, for I am gentle (meek) and humble (lowly) in heart, and you will find rest relief and ease and refreshment and recreation and blessed quiet) for your souls. For My yoke is wholesome (useful, good-not harsh, hard, sharp, or pressing, but comfortable, gracious, and pleasant), and My burden is light and easy to be borne.

Chapter Three

Physical Healer

After the divorce, I moved to California to be closer to my mother and baby sister. When I moved, I still did not trust God enough to go into the ministry full-time as He requested of me. I still had that old mindset of self-survival. I did not just get one job, but two, even though the Spirit of God instructed me to go straight to the pastor at my new church and tell him I was called to preach the gospel and allow him to instruct me on what to do next. We can be very stubborn can't we? I want, I feel, I know we all have that "I" syndrome at times and that does not please God. The jobs took me away from my children, God, and following His instructions for my life. I had no time for the most important people in my life. I stopped going to church every Sunday. I worked three Sundays out of the month. My focus was on paying bills and providing clothing for the children instead of seeking the Kingdom of God first and waiting for all those things to be added unto me. We sometimes forget the principle thing. Matthew 6:33 (KJV) says, *"But seek ye first the kingdom of God, and his*

righteousness; and all these things shall be added unto you."
Seeking the Kingdom of God first means that those who are
believers are to continually seek first God's righteousness.
Once we do that, then all of the material things will come.
Please don't misunderstand me. I'm not saying you should
not work and just wait on God to provide. The Bible says that
if any would not work, neither should he eat (2 Thessa-
lonians 3:10, KJV). I'm advising you to follow the leading of
God. I had two nice jobs that paid the bills, but it was not
like the joy I had when I was obedient to Him. I had also
stopped paying tithes. My Spirit was willing, but my flesh
was weak.

I truly wanted to know Him more and more, but I was
not able to understand at the time that He wanted me to kill
the fleshly desire I was having about the weight I had
gained. I could remember not having peace any longer
because the Holy Spirit was instructing me to go out and do
what I was born to do, but my flesh kept telling me to wait
until I lost the weight. I was deceived into thinking that no
one would listen to what I had to say about Jesus with all
that weight on me. I would think that way because words
are powerful to uplift or bring down. The enemy used the
words my ex-husband said to me when I asked him one day,
right before I completed the divorce papers. I asked, "Do you
love me, and why are we not intimate any longer?" His
respond was, "Look at how big you are; who would want
someone like you? I tried to love you, but I just don't and
never have." The enemy first tries to attack our mind. I
tried for a few months to lose the weight, but nothing was
happening for me. Some of the ladies at my job were going
to the doctor for the gastro bypass surgery. I did not know
what that was the first time I heard about it.

I decided to allow the doctors to do the gastro bypass
surgery. I almost died. Don't misunderstand, it was not the
surgery that almost killed me, it was a lack of listening on
my part. The Holy Spirit, along with family members,

advised me not to have the surgery, but I thought it would allow me to feel more confident while doing the will of my Father in heaven. The world tells us we are not right if we don't look like the Hollywood stars. But let me tell you, when it all boils down and you're on your death bed, believe me, you will not care how you look to anyone but God. I and a few other women got the surgery done around the same time. They all did well. My boss really did not want me to do the procedure. She would walk by and try to talk me out of it. I thought to myself, "Why is she only coming to me and not the others?" I thought it was because I might have been the only one not gossiping about her. They all would talk about how mean she was. Yet, they were the same ones who were late all the time and playing around when they should have been working. I did not recognize the fact that God was using her to get my attention. He will always provide a way out of siding with the enemy, but I wasn't listening to Him.

I know some of you have always done what God told you to do, but I'm sorry to tell you, I was not one of those people; and more likely you're not either, even if you think you are. Well, the day I went for surgery I was excited. I thought to myself finally, 'Finally I'll be back in God's perfect plan for my life when I lose weight.' Well, little did I know, His perfect plan was to have me just as I was. But I thought he was looking at me with human eyes, the same way my ex-husband did. The Lord wants us to come just as we are. The Holy Spirit will make changes inside of us. We are not able to change ourselves into the person God wants us to become. He just wants us to trust Him. I had the surgery and one week later I was back at the hospital. My surgeon gave strict orders before the surgery to come back to him only if I had any problems. He pleaded with me that if things were not going right to come back to him specifically and no other hospital. I went back to see him, but his associate took care of me because my surgeon went on vacation. I stayed in the hospital over two weeks. He had to do surgery on me once again because he could not understand why I could not hold down any food in my stomach. The hospital was not close to home. No one came to visit. When he told me I could go home I just jumped at the chance. He advised me to visit my doctor when he came back from vacation, but I didn't call. I did not want to go back to the hospital anymore. Even though I was not feeling well when I left the hospital, I just thought it was normal. I realize now I was very stubborn and did not follow instructions. We do not know how to follow instructions all the time especially from the Holy Spirit. My doctor's office would call me to come in, but I would just tell them "I will", would even set up an appointment, but would always cancel.

My job always seemed more important than my life at the time. I could not eat or drink anything. It would just come back up. The only thing I could eat was pickles. That should have told me something! One of the ladies who had the surgery before me bought me a huge jar of pickles, so I could just eat something. They all saw that I was killing myself, but I could not see that. I remember sitting at my desk asking God to just let something stay in my stomach. I couldn't even keep water down. I had gotten so weak and dehydrated that I could hardly breathe. Then one day at work, I was walking from the ladies room and dropped to the floor. One of the employees said, "She is one of the ladies that had that surgery." I got angry and shouted out loud, "That is not why I fell; I just tripped!" But there was nothing for me to have tripped on. I just did not want to be in that hospital anymore and I was afraid that was going to happen. So, I got up and acted as though nothing had happened. In addition, I did not tell my family. I was very angry with that lady and myself! I thought foolishly to myself, 'She even has the nerve to help me up after I just yelled at her for trying to suggest I might need help.' I was angry with myself because I let things get so bad and was full of pride; let me tell you pride will kill you. Sometimes we can allow pride to destroy us. This is why God hates the proud, not because He hates us, but He knows that spirit comes from Satan. Remember, Satan comes to steal, kill and destroy. He truly tried to destroy me. It was difficult for me to even get into my van because I had no strength to pull myself up. I remember my children had to give me a push all the time, and my oldest son drove me to work every day because I did not have the strength to even steer the wheel.

I finally made an appointment to see the doctor, but it was too late. One week later, the children and I were talking about the next day and school and were laughing and joking. I went to bed and said good night to my children, but did not wake up the next morning, or the next day. My children saw that I did not get up to work that morning. They just thought I was tired of working because I was laughing with them that night. The next morning, I still did not get up. I just moaned and groaned, but still they thought nothing of it. I stayed in that bed the entire day until the following morning and they said to me, "Mom, we're hungry," but still no response from me. They just stormed out of the room. I couldn't wake up. They just never thought it would happen to their mother. Because it was not my character to miss work without calling and my manager had not heard anything from me, my supervisor was concerned and called my home. When my oldest son could not wake me up, he immediately told her, "She can't wake up and is hardly breathing!" She told him to call 911 while she was on her way to my house. The paramedics came to take me to the hospital. I was delirious, but able to ask my mother not to leave me. After that, I went into a coma.

I slipped in and out of the coma twice a few weeks apart. I do not remember anything after that except while I was in this deep sleep I called the coma, God manifested Himself to me both times. The first time, I was walking at the bottom of the ocean breathing as though it was a normal thing. I did not know at the time that I was in a coma because everything seemed so real. An angelic being was walking beside me. I could only see the flow of the white gown in the water. I knew I was walking in the ocean because I saw different kinds of sea animals I had never seen before. I was not able to look at the face of the angel walking with me, but I felt very safe and a peace that cannot be explained with human words. As we walked there were two very handsome, well-dressed men walking toward us. Immediately, I knew they were evil. With a loud voice I said, "Satan, get behind me!" Without fear I spoke those words as if they were a part of my daily routine. The men just flowed away from the sound of my voice. Immediately, the angelic being spoke to me, saying, "That is how it's supposed to be when you speak in the earth world."

David said to the Lord,

"I take wings of the morning, and dwell in the uttermost part of the sea; Even there shall thy hand lead me, and thy right hand shall hold me.

≈ Psalm 139:9-10, KJV

For truly I say to you, if you have faith [that is living] like a grain of mustard seed, you can say to this mountain, Move from here to yonder place, and it will move; and nothing will be impossible to you.

≈ Matthew 17:20

My mother shared some of the things she had to endure while waiting on the Lord to move. She was on the way to the hospital when God told her to stop and ask a lady, who's son had died in the hospital, to pray for me. This same lady, I thought did not like me. Isn't it funny how God will use the very people you think you have a problem with to help you? Well, this lady told her that she would pray for me, but would not go to the hospital. The lady told me after I came out of the coma, that the same night she could not sleep. God told her to get up in the middle of the morning about 2:00 a.m., clean herself up and go to the hospital and pray for me. She had to come into His presence clean. He instructed her to take my mother a praise CD. She said that when she entered my room she was afraid because she felt the presence of God all around me. As she was praying, she fell back in the chair as though a force shoved her. She left that room and told my mother to play the CD repeatedly. She knew God was protecting me. I remember hearing praise music. I was praising the Lord the entire time the music played. I know I was in a place not of this world! I also know there is an anointing on that CD. While praising Him, there was a light shining on this bench shaped like a judgment seat in the courthouse. I could remember when the song came on about the mercy seat, that I was running and running thinking, 'If I could only make it to the mercy seat on the right side of the judge, everything was going to be alright!' The closer I got the further the seat went. I never could get close to Him. I could just see a figure. The closer I got it seemed the bench would move back further away. I knew that was Jesus sitting in that seat on the right hand of God. I don't know what else I wanted more than to be in His arms. I dropped to the floor and lifted up my hands and praised Him and He came to me. I knew I was in the presence of the Lord.

He informed me that I had not completed the assignment He had planned for my life. I can't remember everything He told me, but I know when it's time He'll reveal all to me once again. For this reason, I had to return to this world. He gave me another chance to get it right, my friend, by being obedient to the Word and will of God—instructing me what to do and say when I returned to His people. God informed me that although there are different denominations, there is only one Church as far as He is concerned and that is the body of Christ. Some people in the church today truly believe they do not have to completely live by the instructions God has laid down in His Word for us. They still fornicate, lie, practice ungodly behavior and do ungodly sexual practices with the same gender, deceive others, etc. This does not exclude those in leadership such as the Apostles, Prophets, Evangelist, Pastors and Teachers. Jesus came to save souls not to destroy them and see them lost and scattered because they are being deceived. 1 John 3:7-8 (KJV) tells us,

Little children, let no man deceive you: he that doeth righteousness is righteous, even as he is righteous. He that committeth sin is of the devil; for the devil sinneth from the beginning. For this purpose the Son of God was manifested, that he might destroy the works of the devil.

Jesus did not do or say anything than what His Father in heaven had told Him. He was without sin.

The doctor went to my mother and advised her that the right side of my heart had stopped beating and wanted to know what she wanted him to do because I was not breathing on my own. She told him that God said I would live, so she believed He would heal my heart. The Holy Spirit had spoken to her and said, "God does not do anything halfway." He had already told her that I would live. They kept coming to tell her so many things that were going wrong: the gray side of my brain was not functioning any longer and my organs were starting to stick to my insides like glue which was a sign of death. She told him that she did not want to hear any more and advised the doctors to do all they could and let God do the rest. She proceeded to tell him what God told her. He just turned and walked away and then turned back and told my mother that whatever she was standing on, he would stand with her. He then started to call her "mother."

When the doctor and my mother both came into agreement with one another, I started getting better. I had woken from the deep sleep (my first coma), and thought to myself, "Why is everyone looking at me with such sadness?" The last thing I remembered was sleeping in my own bed. I saw my oldest sister who lived in another state and wondered why she was in California. I also saw my ex-husband from Chicago with the rest of the family. My mother then told me what had happened to me. I knew then being with Jesus was not a dream because I had returned back to this place. The first thing I asked was, "Did I pay my rent yet?" That was the last thing I remembered I had to pay. I know now why Jesus warned us when He said,

> *"Be careful, or your hearts will be weighed down with dissipation, drunkenness and the anxieties of life, and that day will close on you unexpectedly like a trap. For it will come upon all those who live on the face of the whole earth.*
>
> — Luke 21:34-35, NIV

Instead of worrying about paying a bill, I should have been thanking and praising Him for allowing me to wake up from my coma.

As weeks went by, my sister came to visit me in the hospital. We would laugh about old times. One day, as she was trying to get a urine sample for the doctor, she slipped and fell! We laughed so hard the nurses came running into the room thinking I was having heart failure because the monitors at the front desk were beeping like crazy. They advised my sister of the importance of my heart condition, and she would not be able to stay if she kept on getting me excited. My sister nor I was aware of how serious my illness was.

The lady I spoke of earlier whom my mother had stopped and asked to come to the hospital to pray for me was the same person I once thought did not care for me. She explained to me what happened when God told her to come and pray for me, how God used her and how she felt the presence of God all around my bed as though He was protecting me from something. As she talked, all I could think about was how I could not believe she was the one God used for my well-being. I know now how Satan tries to deceive us in our minds, and how he uses people we don't even know and who haven't done anything at all to harm us! He would use delusions of things that were not really happening to me, and lie to me saying people didn't like me—and they hadn't even known me! He even had the nerve to use a magnifying glass so situations appeared larger and worse than they really were. You start telling yourself that you don't like that person but don't know why. Satan does that to distract you so you won't think about the true enemy which is Satan himself, the devil, the evil one. He is the true enemy who is about to be exposed!

I am a witness of his delusions and now know that they are just lies that he plants in our minds. The lady reassured me saying once again that she had no idea why I was thinking of her in that manner. I then felt compelled to tell her about how distorted my thinking was. Again, she did not know why I felt that way when she did not even know me. This is a good example to all of you readers as to why it is so important that we renew our minds daily. I then proceeded to share with her about what had happened to me with the praise CD God had instructed her to give to my mother for me to listen to. I let her know the only thing I listened to was that praise CD. I was so thankful for her obedience to God to bring the CD because it helped to renew my mind as I praised the Lord the entire time the CD played. Before I continue with my story please allow me to share this revelation Jesus shared with me.

As I was listening to a praise CD one day riding in my car alone, I heard the Lord say to me, "Don't hurt me", so I answered casually, "I won't hurt you, Lord." The Lord said to me again, "Don't hurt me." This time it felt as if someone was sitting in the passenger seat. I then felt my heart beating fast with tears welling up in my eyes and I asked Him, "How would I hurt you?" I thought I was already being faithful to Him. He asked me if I would have intimate relations with someone else in bed if I knew my husband was watching at the foot of the bed with his heart broken. I quickly answered with tears in my eyes, "No! I would never do that!" I was thinking to myself that was so crazy for Him to even ask me that knowing He knew how faithful I was to my ex-husband. He knew I didn't believe in cheating with another man knowing He knows all things. The foolish things we think and say sometimes! He then proceeded to tell me how we as His children hurt Him when we are not lawfully married and feel it's okay to have sexual encounters out of wedlock. He said to me, "Every time that happens, I am the one standing at the foot of the bed watching with a broken heart."

God wants us to know that He is our husband while we are single. All I could do was think of God standing there all those times I was not married having sex with men who were not my lawful husband. My heart felt very heavy and tears could not stop falling from my eyes. Please, hear me when I say He knows what those actions will do to you and His relationship. God doesn't want to lose you and I to any lustful pleasures that desire to only please the flesh which in the end results in death. God is faithful. Stop now and ask His forgiveness and He will forgive you right NOW. Continuing with my story...

My mother said she asked God if I was going to live because the doctors told her I would not. God showed her an angel standing in between the light where I was and the darkness. She said the darkness could not pass that angel no matter how hard it tried. The angel told her I would live and not die, and my mother believed God over what the doctors said. Everyone thought my mother was in denial, but she kept standing on what God had promised her. She told everyone who visited me that if they were going to be crying and not have faith, she would not allow them to see me.

I was in the first coma for a few weeks. When I finally was released from the hospital, I stayed home two or three weeks to recover and then returned to work. I still did not know how serious my illness was. My boss was angry that I came back to work so soon. This was the same boss who did not want me to have the surgery. She also stayed at the hospital with me for some time when I came out of the coma. She would bring my mother food to eat because my mother did not leave me as I had asked her not too. My job held a big breakfast fundraiser to give my family a donation to pay for my rent. They collected over $900.00 in two hours and gave my children and I bags of name-brand foods.

I would like to tell you why it's important to give to your own home church. First, your tithes belong to God. Second, so there can be food and substance to give to God's children when they are in need of it as I once was. I thank God for that church in California because they did not have to help me. I paid no tithes at that time making all that money and it paid off nothing but death.

> *Bring ye all the tithes into the storehouse, that there may be meat in mine house, and prove me now herewith, saith the Lord of hosts, if I will not open you the windows of heaven, and pour you out a blessing, that there shall not be room enough to receive it. And I will rebuke the devourer for your sakes, and he shall not destroy the fruits of your ground; neither shall your vine cast her fruit before the time in the field, saith the Lord of hosts.*
>
> Malachi 3:10-11, KJV

I was not at work longer than one week before I went into another coma for the second time. Just like the first time, I was sitting in the front room of my house on the couch talking to my children before bed. It was late and I was thinking about what I would wear to work the next day. We do not know what tomorrow will bring. The Bible says, *"Do not boast about tomorrow, for we do not know what a day may bring forth"* (Proverbs 27:1). This is why it is important for us not to go to bed angry. You do not know when it's your last time to see that person. That night, I said good night to my children and told them I would see them in the morning. Again, I did not wake up! I did not wake up this time for over a month. My mother thought it was best to send away my twins to stay with family members, sell all my things and give up the house that I was renting. They sold just about everything for money. My mother did what she thought was best. My two oldest sons and baby girl stayed in California. They needed to have a place to stay. I would have done the same if I had been in her shoes. These were difficult decisions, this time it was worst then before.

While I was in the coma for the second time, I saw myself back in that long hall with light shining down on the Judgment Seat of God.. This time I did not hear any music, but I still saw myself worshipping God. I did not speak. He was the only one talking. I just listened. The amazing feeling I felt was unexplainable! Being in the presence of the Lord and His glory was amazing! I had no worries, pain or fear. I could not remember having any problems, heartache or pain. The Bible says,

> *And God shall wipe away all tears from their eyes;*
> *and there shall be no more death, neither sorrow,*
> *nor crying, neither shall there be any more pain: for*
> *the former things are passed away.*

> ⟿ Revelation 21:4

God told me that I had to go back and why I could not stay: I had not completed my assignment to go and preach and teach His people how to live by every Word of God. I also had to live by every word in order for me to teach someone else how to do so. God reminded me of the parable in the Bible of the rich man and Lazarus. The word "Father" stated in the scripture below with a capital "F" represents Jesus, and the word" Child" represents those who say Jesus is their Lord and God.

There was a certain rich man who [habitually] clothed himself in purple and fine linen and reveled and feasted and made merry in splendor every day. And at his gate there was [carelessly] dropped down and left a certain utterly destitute man named Lazarus, [reduced to begging alms and] covered with [ulcerated] sores. He [eagerly] desired to be satisfied with what fell from the rich man's table; moreover, the dogs even came and licked his sores. And it occurred that the man [reduced to] begging died and was carried by the angels to Abraham's bosom. The rich man also died and was buried. And in Hades (the realm of the dead), being in torment, he lifted up his eyes and saw Abraham far away, and Lazarus in his bosom. And he cried out and said, Father Abraham, have pity and mercy on me and send) Lazarus to dip the tip of his finger in water and cool my tongue, for I am in anguish in this flame. But Abraham said, Child, remember that you in your lifetime fully received [what is due you in] comforts and delights, and Lazarus in like manner the discomforts and distresses; but now he is comforted here and you are in anguish. And besides all this, between us and you a great chasm has been fixed, in order that those who want to pass from this [place] to you may not be able, and no one may pass from there to us. And [the man] said, them, father, I beseech you to send him to my father's house. For I have five brothers—so that he may give [solemn] testimony and warn them, lest they too come into this place of torment. But Abraham said, they have Moses and the Prophets; let them hear and listen to them. But he answered, No, father Abraham, but if someone from the dead goes to them, they will repent (change their minds for the better and heartily amend their ways, with abhorrence of their past sins). He said to him If they

*do not hear and listen to Moses and the Prophets,
neither will they be persuaded and convinced and
believe [even] if someone should rise from the dead.*

— Luke 16:19-31

Jesus instructed me to look closely at the fact that the
rich man called Abraham "Father" and Abraham called him
his "Child." At the time Jesus was telling this parable, He
was talking to the Jews who were God's chosen people. They
believed they were the seed (children) of Abraham. This is
why Jesus told them who were the true descendants of
Abraham.

*Then said Jesus to those Jews which believed on
him, "If ye continue in my word, then are ye my
disciples indeed; and ye shall know the truth, and
the truth shall make you free." They answered him,
"We be Abraham's seed, and were never in bondage
to any man: how sayest thou, 'Ye shall be made
free'?" Jesus answered them, "Verily, verily, I say
unto you, whosoever committeth sin is the servant of
sin. And the servant abideth not in the house for
ever: but the Son abideth ever. If the Son therefore
shall make you free, ye shall be free indeed. I know
that ye are Abraham's seed; but ye seek to kill me,
because my word hath no place in you. I speak that
which I have seen with my Father: and ye do that
which ye have seen with your father." They
answered and said unto him, "Abraham is our
father." Jesus saith unto them, "If ye were
Abraham's children, ye would do the works of
Abraham. But now ye seek to kill me, a man that
hath told you the truth, which I have heard of God:
this did not Abraham. Ye do the deeds of your
father." Then said they to him, "We be not born of
fornication; we have one Father, even God." Jesus
said unto them, "If God were your Father, ye would
love me: for I proceeded forth and came from God;
neither came I of myself, but he sent me. Why do ye*

*not understand my speech? Even because ye cannot
hear my word. Ye are of your father the devil, and
the lusts of your father ye will do. He was a
murderer from the beginning, and abode not in the
truth, because there is no truth in him. When he
speaketh a lie, he speaketh of his own, for he is a
liar, and the father of it. And because I tell you the
truth, ye believe me not. Which of you convinceth me
of sin? And if I say the truth, why do ye not believe
me? He that is of God heareth God's words: ye
therefore hear them not, because ye are not of God."*

John 8:31-47

He also let me know that there are people who claim to
be followers of Christ Jesus, but do not follow His
instructions. They truly believe they are saved, just like the
rich man did. He called Abraham "father" and Abraham
called him "son." The Lord let me know that the Word of
God will stand and not change. Jesus said,

*Not every one that saith unto me, Lord, Lord, shall
enter into the kingdom of heaven; but he that doeth
the will of my Father which is in heaven. Many will
say to me in that day, Lord, Lord, have we not
prophesied in they name? and in thy name have
cast out devils? And in thy name done many
wonderful works? And then will I profess unto
them, I never knew you: depart from me, ye that
work iniquity.*

Matthew 7:21-23

I pray you are able to hear me when I say the Lord sent
me back to warn everyone who is willing to listen to me that
we are to live by every word of God and tell them that hell is
as real as heaven and we must choose where we want to
spend eternity. Don't allow anyone to tell you anything other
than the Word of God; I tell you the truth as I know it. We
have the Bible so go and read it for yourself because we all
will stand before God alone on Judgment Day.

If you do not obey the Word of God you will not be saved. Jesus gave us a command to love one another. Roman 13:8 states,

> *Keep out of debt and owe no man anything, except to love one another; for he who loves his neighbor [who practices loving others] has fulfilled the Law [relating to one's fellowmen, meeting all its requirements]."*

Faith without works is dead. I must make things clear because God is not the author of confusion. God does not wish anyone to be lost. Hosea 4:6 says,

> *My people are destroyed for lack of knowledge; because you [the priestly nation] have rejected knowledge, I will also reject you that you shall be no priest to Me; seeing you have forgotten the law of your God, I will also forget your children.*

David said, *If I ascend up into heaven, thou art there; if I make my bed in hell, behold, thou art there* (Psalm 139:8). Let us not overlook the words "If I." We have a choice. He created hell for the devil and those who do evil. 2 Peter 2:4-6 tells us,

> *For God did not [even] spare angels that sinned, but cast them into hell, delivering them to be kept there in pits of gloom till the judgment and their doom. And He spared not the ancient world, but preserved Noah, a preacher of righteousness, with seven other persons, when He brought a flood upon the world of ungodly [people]. And He condemned to ruin and extinction the cities of Sodom and Gomorrah, reducing them to ashes [and thus] set them forth as an example to those who would be ungodly.*

We have a choice! God says,

> *I call heaven and earth to witness this day against you that I have set before you life and death. The*

*blessings and the curses; therefore choose life, that
you and your descendants may live.*

☞ Deuteronomy 30:19

I know some will say, "God just has disobedient
children...there's a difference between being disobedient
and refusing to follow the Word of God." Go back and read
what the Word of God has to say about obedience and
disobedience. The Word doesn't lie. Reader, God is talking
to you, not just your friends or family members. It does not
matter whether you're an Apostle, Prophet, Evangelist, or
Pastor and Teacher, He's talking to you!

When I finally awoke from the second coma, I was not
able to breathe on my own, speak, walk, lift my hands to
write, eat, sit up in a chair to watch TV, nor could I see
anything clearly. Everything was a blur. I remember every
night after I had awakened, my mother would leave my
room and a nurse would come and lay a baby at the foot of
my bed. When the morning would come she would politely
come and remove the child. This went on until they
transferred me to another hospital by helicopter. I needed to
have the surgery performed by my doctor in Fresno,
reversed. At the time, I did not understand what the child
represented who was lying at the end of my bed every night,
but I knew there was a message there for me from God. So
I prayed for the understanding of the revelation. Please
remain spiritually focused as you continue to read. This is
very important because the Holy Spirit is writing this book
through me. The Bible tells us that I AM is Spirit, therefore,
you must be in the spirit to understand what He's saying to
you. Believe me; there is a message here just for you! The
Bible also tells us that faith is the things hoped for and the
evidence of things not seen. You may be thinking, "This is
not for me," but if you're reading this book, then it is for you!
You will get what God wants you to receive. Anything from
God is good. God is faithful to those who believe. I was

52

informed by God while writing this book that the baby represented newness, new life, new beginning, new desires, new love, and a new relationship with Him. This might sound like a little too much for some people, but God is faithful to us and desires to bless us with abundance in all ways. He will turn what Satan meant to destroy us into a wonderful testimony meant to edify Himself. I truly believe that because the person who went into the coma was not the same person who awakened from the coma.

My mother came with me to the other hospital, but the people there did not know her and made her sleep outside in the cold. Little did they know she was not going to leave my side! I still was not able to talk without a voice box or move. My doctor who performed the surgery heard from the other hospital that my mother was not going to leave so he asked if she could stay in the hospital. He was wonderful! He treated my mother like a queen while she was there.

God placed good people in my path at that hospital—two nurses in particular. I remember many who helped me. One nurse would dance for me every time she came into my room and that made me want to try and move with her. She would uplift my spirit and make me feel as though I would be alright. I remember when they were moving me from her floor. She said, "When you get out of this place, we are going to go dancing." The other nurse asked her why she would say that knowing that I might never walk again. I could not talk, but I could hear everything. I was feeling upbeat when one positive nurse was speaking positively over my future, but when I heard the other nurse speak negatively, my hopes fell and I could only remember thinking, "I will never dance again" as tears brimmed in my eyes as I tried not to let them see me cry.

God is faithful! He sent another nurse to my room. She saw how down I looked. My mother told her that I had quit smiling. The nurse proceeded to share her testimony with me that she herself was in a wheelchair for nine years. One day, God told her that she could walk, but she did not believe Him. Once again, that same voice told her to get up and walk. This time she listened and obeyed. She's been walking every since. I will never forget those two nurses that spoke life. They are a reminder to me how important the words are which we speak out of our mouths. The Bible says, *"Death and life are in the power of the tongue"* (Proverbs 18:21, KJV).

> *We all stumble in many ways. If anyone is never at fault in what he says, he is a perfect man, able to keep his whole body in check. When we put bits into the mouth of horses we make them obey us. We can turn the whole animal.*
>
> James 3:2-3, NIV

These scriptures tell me that anyone who is unable to tame their tongue is not yet perfect. If we could just tame our tongue, we would be able to keep the whole body from sinning against God. *"Out of the same mouth come praise and cursing. My brothers this should not be"* (James 3:10, NIV).

I turned to look at my mother with a big smile on my face and she knew that I had received that in my spirit and soul. Again, we know that Satan comes to kill, steal and destroy. Instead of getting better and having the reversal surgery, I got worse. Pneumonia developed in my chest and I had to go back on the respirator. Once again, I could not breathe on my own once again. When I was feeling stronger they preceded with the reversal of the surgery. It was successful. After I had recovered from the surgery, the hospital was going to transfer me to a rehabilitation facility. They were concerned that the reason I was not able to walk or sit in a chair on my own was due to having been in the hospital for so long. My mother prayed because she did not want me in a rehabilitation center where she would not be able to stay with me. Believe me, God has His own plans for our lives. Right before it was time for me to leave, I got sick again which lasted for another few weeks. One night, my doctor came to the hospital because they told him I was experiencing internal bleeding. Blood was flowing from somewhere inside my body. He told my mother they would have to run more tests to find out where the bleeding was coming from. As always, my mother started to pray and anoint me with oil. She would not allow anyone to take me away for any test until she would anoint me. I know that I was the oiliest person in the hospital! All tests showed no bleeding. They said it must have dried up somehow, but we all know that prayer works.

Later, my doctor told me that something told him to go to the hospital and check on me. He was surprised to find me going into shock. I remember wondering why everyone was yelling, "Stay with us...don't go to sleep!" I was calmly looking at them and thinking, "I'm fine...what's going on?" The next morning I woke up to see my doctor sitting in the chair just watching me. He said, "You gave me a scare last night." I did not know what he was talking about because I was feeling just fine. They could not find any blood nor heart problems that caused me to go into shock. After that, I came down with shingles. I could not leave until it went away. That gave time for the doctor to assign physical therapy for me for at least a few weeks to see if I could show some kind of improvement. This allowed my mother to take me home and have hospice come to the home. It was a big challenge just for me to try to sit up. I want you to know that it was not just physically difficult for me; it was also difficult to think. I had to be trained to speak and to write again. This illness truly was a challenge for my faith in God.

Well, it was time for me to start walking. God would have me walk around the hospital every day in the spirit world. When the therapist would come to my room to help me sit up, I would tell them I had walked already and they should just leave me alone because I was tired of walking. I remember they would just look at me and smile telling me to show them how I walked around the hospital and which way I went. But I could not even sit up to show them. I started to think I was going crazy or something because it was just so real to me.

My mother would look at me as I would tell those physical therapists the same thing when they would come. I saw myself in gym shoes and told them about the shoes. I said, "So you will know I'm telling the truth, just look at the shoes in the closet that I wear every time I walk, since you don't believe I can get up." They looked in the closet to show me that I was only imagining things. I started to cry because I knew it was real and no one would believe me. I did not know what was going on. My mother waited until they left the room and started to ask questions like, "Why would you think you could walk when you can't even keep your balance?" She gave me something to think about and told me to ask God what He was showing me because I know she knew I was not just being lazy and didn't want to walk. I truly believed that I had walked. I asked God the next time He showed me that vision or dream, "Did I walk?" I sounded just like a child asking his father a question. He responded to me and said, "Yes, but not in this world." He said that I had to see myself walking in the spirit first before I could walk in the natural. I told my mother what He said and asked her to get the gym shoes I had seen in the spirit. I understood in the spirit that the shoes would give me balance. She believed me and went and bought me some gym shoes.

Every day, twice a day, my doctor assigned the physical therapists to walk with me so that I could go home. My approach in getting ready for them changed after I spoke to God for a little while. It was hard and painful. Even with pain pill, I would cry. The pain was so unbearable I could hardly breathe. The therapists would pull a chair behind me because I was only able to take two steps before I would have to sit down. I had no energy. As they continued to work with me, I was able to walk to the door and back to the bed without sitting in the chair. My mother would encourage me all the time when I wanted to give up. She was so determined. She would not take "no" for an answer. She continually reminded me of what God had told me. The physical therapist would come and ask if I felt up to walking that day. I would say, "Not today, come back tomorrow." Some days I did not want to feel the pain, but my mother knew the importance of me walking every day as the doctor had ordered. They would go and tell my mother I refused to walk today. I would see her coming after they left the room and think to myself, "Here she comes again...I know she's going to make me walk." I would become angry. My doctor was even angrier with the therapists for allowing me to choose not to walk. So he informed them that if I didn't get up and walk when they came, that they should go and tell my mother. The next time they came, I thought they were leaving because I said no, but they just went to tell on me. I truly thank God for the doctors at both hospitals because they did not give up on me. They were persistent with me and my mother would not give up either. I also thank God for those two therapists who were working with me. They did not give up either.

After a few weeks of therapy, I was able to walk with assistance. I could not walk alone, but was doing well enough that I was able to go home with my mother and continue therapy there. I will never forget when I was leaving the hospital that God reminded me of the prayer I had prayed to Him when I said, "Please allow me to go outside and hear the birds tweeting." That was the best music I had ever heard. I can say now we sometimes take for granted the beauty of nature God has given to us. To this day, I still love the sound of the birds singing early in the morning.

When I got home, I was still not able to keep my balance or go to the restroom by myself. I would sit on the couch listening to a television set that I couldn't see due to my blurry vision. I was still asking God why He sent me back to earth. It's hard for some people to understand why I would ask such a question, but if you had experienced how beautiful the feeling was when I was with Him, you would ask that same question. I can say that during my recovery I acted like a very stubborn child. God continued to say, "You have not completed your assignment yet." My mother heard me talking to God with a tone of anger and demanded that I never speak to Him that way again. She thought it was disrespectful. I cried like a baby because my mind was still like a child's. I had to start all over again in so many ways.

When my mother would go out for business, my sons had to stay and care for me. They would take me to the restroom and turn their heads because they had to pull down my pants and sit me on the toilet. They never complained. I knew it was hard for them to see me like that, but they did it and would not allow me to see them cry. I had to move in with my mother and her friend she was renting a room from. It was hard for me to not be able to go home. I couldn't walk, talk or see well. I had to share a bed with my mother. It was not easy for either of us.

The therapist came about three times a week. I had to have blood drawn daily to check my sugar and I was on Coumadin, a blood thinner. I had no feeling in my feet. Every night I would see Jesus massaging my legs and feet. I could even see the blood going through my body to my feet as though He was pushing it through. I saw this until it manifested. I started to feel sensation in my legs and feet. It felt like pins sticking me in my feet. I will always remember what the Holy Spirit told me in the hospital. He told me that I must see it happening in the spirit in order for it to manifest in the natural. When the therapist came, she would tell me to lift my legs while I watched television, but

I would always say, "I can't, I can't do it!" The Holy Spirit would tell me to say nothing and just do it. Even though, in the natural, I couldn't. But in the spirit, I could see myself doing it. A few weeks went by and it seemed as though nothing was going on, then one night my feet just started burning like they were on fire. I tried to cool them off by touching the floor. I did not realize that I had not been able to feel and that this was a good thing. My mother knew something was happening. During my next appointment with the therapist, she suggested that I try walking while holding a pot. The distance from the sink to the refrigerator was only a couple of feet. I did not want to do it, but I did and kept on doing it while remembering what the Holy Spirit had said.

One morning I called for my mother to help me into the bathroom. She did not come. She said, "You can do it yourself...just hold onto the wall and you can do it!" I started to cry and feel sorry for myself but she refused to come to my rescue. When I was finished crying, the Holy Spirit said, "You can do it." I responded, "I will fall if I try that because I can't hold myself up." The Holy Spirit then said, "If you believe that, then you're right." That is all He said. My mother yelled from the kitchen and said to me, "If you wet your pants you will have even more work to do!" I knew she was not going to come, so I started to ask God to help me up. All He was waiting for was for me to ask Him, believe and do it without fear. Mark 11:23-24 says,

> *Truly I tell you, whoever says to this mountain, Be lifted up and thrown into the sea! And does not doubt at all in his heart but believes that what he says will take place; it will be done for him. For this reason I am telling you, whatever you ask for in prayer, believe (trust and be confident) that it is granted to you, and you will [get it]. That was my first step with God's guidance. I then knew, nothing was impossible for God, even though the doctors say no, but God said yes.*

Luke 18:27 also says, "The things which are impossible with men are possible with God."

I began to walk with a walker. It was not an easy task. People would stare at me when I walked by. I used to wonder what they were thinking. Did they wonder why I was using the walker at such a young age? Did they wonder what happened to me? I would hate it when people would come out and ask me because I was ashamed to tell them. I knew it was my disobedience to God's call to preaching His Word. I didn't want to explain how I wanted to wait until I was small enough to preach. All I could remember was asking God, "If you would just allow me to gain some weight, I will never dislike myself again." Believe me when I tell you, that is the first time I ever thought of praying to gain weight!

Chapter Four

Provider

I now want to share how God provided for me when I had to move from my mother's friend's home. She gave me two weeks to find an apartment. Don't misunderstand me, she was a very sweet lady and I truly believe she wanted the best for me and my children. This was God's doing to try my faith in Him. The neighbors were telling her all kinds of things about my boys that were not true, but she did not know who to believe. She had known them for very long time. I was staying with her while going through this ordeal. My mother left and moved to Chicago and took care of my grandmother until she died of cancer. I was left to find an apartment for myself and the two oldest boys along with my baby girl that stayed in California with me. They would go out and talk to their friends not knowing what to do. The lady I was currently living with felt bad about asking me to move, but that's what she really wanted. I would tell her not to worry about me because I knew God did not send me back just to be left out on the street. The last night I stayed at her home, I found out that one of my son's friend's father had a house going up for rent in a few days. But his daughter knew my situation and told my son I could have that apartment. They wanted me to meet with them, but I told them no because I was not able to travel alone without a car. She came to me at 9:00 that night. I never gave up believing God was going to provide for me and my children.

I was told I could move in the very next day. It was a small place, but I didn't care. I just kept praising the Lord for providing a place for me and my children. The apartment had one bedroom, a small kitchen, a small living room and one bathroom close to the living room. Sometimes we don't appreciate what we have until we have something worse or it's gone. I stayed there for one year until my son graduated from high school, then I decided to move to Memphis, Tennessee. But the Lord commanded me to move to St. Louis, Missouri. My mother and other family members did not want me to move there. Upon arrival, my birth father lived in St. Louis and came out and asked me why I had really moved there. I told him the Lord had sent me. I don't think he believed me because he thought I came to get something from him. I'm telling you this because you must always do what God tells you, no matter what others might believe or think about you and your past. God will never command you to do something and not provide what you need to accomplish it.

I lived with my father for a few weeks and immediately started looking for a place to live. It was crowded in his home for me and my three children. The first place we looked at was a disaster. It was filthy and had no running water. You could see the thick dust in the air. It was not livable, but I told God if I had to sleep outdoors and have no place for my children to lay their heads, I was still going to stay in St. Louis and trust Him to find me a place. I wrote the man a check and before I got home, my cousin called and asked me to come and look at one of his houses; I did not remember him living in St. Louis until he called me. God wanted me to trust Him first, and then He had my cousin call and say he had a place for me. I went over to take a look at the house and my children fell in love with that place. My cousin had not yet seen me, so he thought I still could not walk up and down stairs. I told God that I would not take the walker or the cane to St. Louis with me because I believed He was going to heal me completely.

After I got settled, I joined the church that God instructed me to join, New Jerusalem. I did not know Natalie the Sunday school superintendent I spoke about earlier in the story. She's the lady God said I would be trained under, remember? She was now the first lady of that church and married the senior pastor who was a friend of my family. I did not know they lived there until my mother reminded me of them living in St. Louis. The Lord reminded me that He had told me I would be trained under this woman about 15 years ago. I had never felt so peaceful or happy in my life. I had never tried to be as obedient to God's commandments like I was then. I know I returned to this body a different person! After sitting under my pastor for about two years, I finally went to him and told him I was called to the ministry. I gave him a recording, instructed by God because he seemed as if he was too busy to sit and talk with me. He listened to the tape. When we met, I explained what my instructions were from God, but he knew already. He said that he was just waiting for me to come to him. I explained why I didn't go to him until God said it was time. I acknowledged Him in all my decisions. My pastor asked when I wanted to give my first sermon. I told him I would allow God to advise him on that. Once he heard from God, he should let me know.

He came to me a few months later and told me that the Lord said it was time. He chose December 9th as the date for my first sermon. I was so excited! I remembered my mother always said to wait for God and He would make room for my gift in His time. This was not an easy decision for my pastor. He was pastoring in a place where they don't believe women are called to preach the gospel. Some of the members thought they owned the church since they had been there for so long and were longtime members of the Board. Some even went so far as to go to the pastor and tell him they would not allow it and felt he was going against God. People sometimes think they should assist God like Saul (Paul) did by persecuting Jesus; by putting Christians in jail. Acts 9:1-2 says,

> *Meanwhile Saul, still drawing his breath hard from threatening and murderous desire against the disciples of the Lord, went to the high priest And requested of him letters to the synagogues at Damascus [authorizing him], so that if he found any men or women belonging to the Way [of life as determined by faith in Jesus Christ], he might bring them bound [with chains] to Jerusalem.*

Who sends forth His disciples to do His will? Is it the Father's will for all to hear the Good News? God is looking for a willing vessel, not a gender.

When the time came for me to preach my first sermon, I went to look for a particular Bible at a local retail store because I could not find it at any of the Christian bookstores. I wanted that Bible so that I could prepare a message. My pastor would ask me every Sunday, "What do you have?" I had nothing in my mind, but I always had it in my heart; what God wanted me to preach on. I didn't just want to sound like any another preacher. I wanted to change lives and save souls. "Wow! While I was at the retail store, a lady came to me and started trying to help me. She showed me all kinds of books, except the Bible I was looking for. She asked if I had read this or that and would tell me how great they were. I told her I was looking for a particular Bible called "The Answer." God had told me to purchase one before and give it to another lady who could not afford to purchase the

Bible at that time. There was only one Bible and God told me to get it for her. I then started looking for the same Bible every place I would go. The woman who helped me worked as a demo lady passing out pastry samples. She was very friendly and asked me a question, "Why are you looking so hard for this Bible?" I told her I had to preach my first sermon the next day. She held both my hands looking me straight in the eyes with a warm smile and said these powerful words, "the best sermon comes from the heart... don't you know that?" I then smiled knowing that came from Jesus. God was letting me know it was going to be okay...to trust Me.

I stopped looking for that Bible and went home praising God for that woman God used to speak to my spirit. I must say, I truly believe she was sent just for me from above. My pastor asked me that Sunday morning if I was ready to preach my first sermon that evening. I have never felt so nervous before in all my life. To make things worse, there was another pastor who had been preaching for more than forty years who informed my pastor that he did not believe in women preaching the gospel. Satan made sure that I overheard him in the other room right before it was time for me to preach. This preacher taught that women are to be silent in church.

> *Let your women keep silence in the churches: for it is not permitted unto them to speak; but they are commanded to be under obedience, as also saith the law.*
>
> 1 Corinthians 14:34

It was always amazing to me that they never explained that verse when teaching; explain why and what the Corinthians were doing for Paul to write to their church about that issue. The apostle Paul knew they needed order in the church and everyone was speaking out of turn during the service. Some of the women were dishonoring their husbands. That is why Paul goes on to say that these women should ask their own husband questions at home instead of interrupting the service. 1 Corinthians 11:11-12 tells us:

> *Nevertheless, in [the plan of] the Lord and from His point of view woman is not apart from and independence of man, nor is man aloof from and independence of woman; For as woman was made from man, even so man is also born of woman; and all [whether male of female go forth] from God [as their Author].*

Paul had many women helping him in the church. (Read Philippians 4:3, Acts 9:36-41, 16:14-15, Romans 16:9, and 16:12-13). God used a woman named Deborah, who was a prophetess, to judge Israel (Judges 4:4-23).

I preached the sermon from Luke 16:27-31—the one God instructed me to preach while I was in the coma. I might never meet many of you that are reading this book, so I pray that you receive the testimony of my life from the Lord who inspired me to write this book. No one knows the day or the hour Jesus, the Son of Man, will return. In Matthew 24:36-44, Jesus says,

> *No one knows about the day or the hour, not even the angels in heaven, nor the Son, but only the Father. As it was in the days of Noah, so it will be at the days of the coming of the Son of Man. For in the days before the flood, people were eating and drinking, marrying and giving in marriage, up to the day Noah entered the ark: and they knew nothing about what would happen until the flood came and took them all away. That is how it will be at the coming of the Son of Man. Two men will be in the field: one will be taken and the other left. Two women will be grinding with a hand mill; one will be taken and the other left. "Therefore keep watch because you do not know on what day your Lord will come. But understand this: if the owner of*

the house had known at what time of night the thief was coming, he would have kept watch and would not have let his house be broken into. So you also must be ready because the Son of Man will come at an hour when you do not expect him.

The apostle Peter writes to the Church to remind us of the Day of the Lord:

Dear friends, this is now my second letter to you. I have written both of them as reminders to stimulate you to wholesome thinking. I want you to recall the words spoken in the past by the holy prophets and the command given by our Lord and Savior through your apostles. First of all, you must understand that in the last days scoffers (mockers) will come, scoffing (mocking) and following their own evil desires. They will say, "Where is this coming he promised? Ever since our fathers died, everything goes on as it has since the beginning of creation." But they deliberately forget that long ago by God's word the heavens existed and the earth was formed out of water and by water. By these waters also the world of that time was deluged and destroyed. By the same word the present heavens and earth are reserved for fire, being kept for the day of judgment and destruction of ungodly men. But do not forget this one thing, dear friends: With the Lord a day is like a thousand years, and a thousand years are like a day.

2 Peter 3:1-8, NIV

Believe me when I say to you, not everyone who call Jesus "Lord" will enter into the kingdom of heaven. The Bible is true and the Lord will know us by our fruit:

Not everyone who says to me, Lord, Lord, will enter the kingdom of heaven, but only he who does the will of my Father who is in heaven. Many will say to me that day, "Lord, Lord, did we not prophesied in your name and in your name drive out demons

*and perform many miracles?" Then I will tell them
plainly, I never knew you. Away from me, you
evildoers!*

⇒ Matthew 7:21-23

What He is saying is that the fruit you produce while on
earth can be evil! Know what kind of fruit you are producing
in this lifetime. This is what's going to matter when
Judgment Day comes and we stand before God. Galatians
5:22-26 states:

> *But the fruit of the [Holy] Spirit [the work which
> His presence within accomplishes] is love, joy
> (gladness), peace, patience (an even temper,
> forbearance), kindness, goodness (benevolence),
> faithfulness, Gentleness (meekness, humility), self-
> control (self-restraint, continence). Against such
> things there is no law [that can bring a charge].
> And those who belong to Christ Jesus (the Messiah)
> have crucified the flesh (the godless human nature)
> with its passions and appetites and desires. If we
> live by the [Holy] Spirit, let us also walk by the
> Spirit. [If by the Holy Spirit we have our life in
> God, let us go forward walking in line, our conduct
> controlled by the spirit.] Let us not become
> vainglorious and self-conceited, competitive and
> challenging and provoking and irritating to one
> another, envying and being jealous of one another.*

Ephesians 4:4-7 informs us that:

> *[There is] one body and one Spirit—just as there is
> also one hope [that belongs] to the calling you
> receive— [There is] one Lord, one faith, one
> baptism, One God and Father of [us] all, Who is
> above all [Sovereign over all], pervading all and
> [living] in [us] all, Yet grace (God's unmerited
> favor) was given to each of us individually [not
> indiscriminately, but in different ways] in
> proportion to the measure of Christ's [rich and
> bounteous] gift.*

God is the one who chooses the gifts and talents we all possess, so don't think more highly of yourself than you should. We can do nothing without Him! Well, Jesus did not come to destroy the law, but fulfilled it (Matthew 5:17).

Personal Invitation

To those of you who have not yet accepted Jesus as your Lord and Savior, do not be deceived thinking that God will lead and guide you without accepting His Son, Jesus Christ first. You must allow Him to come into your heart and become the head of your life. He is now calling you to Himself. Matthew 11:28-30 says,

Come to Me, all you who labor and are heavy-laden and overburdened, and I will cause you to rest. [I will ease and relieve and refresh your souls.] Take My yoke upon you and learn of Me, for I am gentle (meek) and humble (lowly) in heart, and you will find rest (relief and ease and refreshment and recreation and blessed quiet) for your souls. For My yoke is wholesome (useful, good—not harsh, hard, sharp, or pressing, but comfortable, gracious, and pleasant), and My burden is light and easy to be borne.

Romans 10:9-10 tells us,

For with the heart a person believes (adheres to, trusts in, and relies on Christ) and so is justified

(declared righteous, acceptable to God), and with the mouth he confesses (declares openly and speaks out freely his faith) and confirms [his] salvation."

This is all you need to do to become a child of God.

If you acknowledge and confess with your lips that Jesus is Lord and in your heart believe (adhere to, trust in, and rely on the truth) that God raised Him from the dead, you will be saved. For with the heart a person believes (adheres to, trusts in and relies on Christ) and so is justified (declared righteous, acceptable to God), and with the mouth he confesses (declares openly and speaks out freely his faith) and confirms [his] salvation.

Ephesians 2:7-8

Revelation 3:20-22 says,

Behold, I stand at the door and knock; if anyone hears and listens to and heeds My voice and opens the door, I will come in to him and will eat with him, and he [will eat] with Me. He who overcomes (is victorious), I will grant him to sit beside Me on My throne, as I Myself overcame (was victorious) and sat down beside My Father on His throne. He who is able to hear, let him listen to and heed what the [Holy] Spirit says to the assemblies (churches).

Faith Verses

If you need to build your faith, meditate on and confess these verses daily:

Now faith is being sure of what we hope for and certain of what we do not see...and without faith it is impossible to please God because anyone who comes to him must believe that he exists and that he rewards those who earnestly seek him.

— Hebrews 11:1,6

But when he asks, he must believe and not doubt because he who doubts is like a wave of the sea, blown and tossed by the wind.

— James 1:6

So that your faith might not rest on men's wisdom, but on God's power.

— 1 Corinthians 2:5

But what does it say? "The word is near you; it is in your mouth and in your heart," that is, the word of faith we are proclaiming. Consequently, faith comes from hearing the message, and the message is heard through the word of Christ.

◈ Romans 10:8,17

I tell you the truth, if anyone says to this mountain, "Go, throw yourself into the sea," and does not doubt in his heart but believes that what he says will happen, it will be done for him...Therefore I tell you, whatever you ask for in prayer, believe that you have received it, and it will be yours.

◈ Mark 11:23,24

Yet he did not waver through unbelief regarding the promise of God, but was strengthened in his faith and gave glory to God, being full persuaded that God had power to do what he had promised.

◈ Romans 4:20,21

Clearly no one is justified before God by the law because, "The righteous will live by faith."

◈ Galatians 3:11

In addition to all this, take up the shield of faith, with which you can extinguish all the flaming arrows of the evil one.

◈ Ephesians 6:16

Know the True You!

For nothing is impossible with God.

~ Luke 1:37

What is impossible with men is possible with God."

~ Luke 18:27

And those he predestined, he also called, those he called, he also justified; those he justified, he also glorified. What then, shall we say in response to this? If God is for us, who can be against us?

~ Romans 8:30-31

But you are a chosen people, a royal priesthood, a holy nation, a people belonging to God, that you may declare the praises of Him who called you out of darkness into His wonderful light.

~ 1 Peter 2:9

For we are God's workmanship, created in Christ Jesus to do good works, which God prepared in advance for us to do.

~ Ephesians 2:10

Seleria not able to walk without assistance.

Therapist teaching Seleria how to gain balance to stand alone.

To contact the author, please write her at:

P.O. Box 150106
St. Louis, MO 63115

www.evangelistseleriaperryman.com
www.facetofaceministriesinc.net
email: seleriap@yahoo.com

CPSIA information can be obtained at www.ICGtesting.com
Printed in the USA
LVOW131822080712

289147LV00001B/7/P

9 781593 523176